Faithful Footsteps: Navigating Parenthood with Faith

patrick maina

Published by patoh, 2024.

Table of Contents

Faithful Footsteps: Navigating Parenthood with Faith

Table of Contents

Introduction:

The Christian Parenting Journey Begins

PART I: LAYING THE FOUNDATION

PART II: SHAPING CHARACTER AND VIRTUE

PART V: SPECIAL CIRCUMSTANCES AND RELATIONSHIPS

Chapter 17: Parenting Special Needs Children with Grace

Chapter 18: Strengthening Marital Bonds in Christian Parenting

Chapter 19: The Legacy of Faithful Parenting

Conclusion: Empowering Families with Faith

INTRODUCTION:

Welcome to "Faithful Footsteps: Navigating Parenthood with Faith," a transformational handbook that goes into the heart of Christian parenting. In a world full of uncertainties, raising children grounded in faith offers a beacon of hope and direction. This book is your companion on the remarkable journey of nurturing not only the minds and hearts of your children but their souls as well.

The role of a Christian parent is more than just providing physical care, academic support, and material comforts. It is a calling, a vocation, and a ministry rooted in the teachings of Jesus Christ. As Christian parents, we are entrusted with the divine responsibility of nurturing our children's hearts, minds, and souls, helping them grow in the knowledge and love of God.

Join us as we embark on this sacred journey together, learning to walk in faith and imparting that faith to the next generation. With God's wisdom lighting our path, we can navigate the beautiful complexities of parenthood with grace and confidence.

Acknowledgment

First and foremost, I thank God for His unwavering guidance and grace throughout this journey. Without His light, this book would not have been possible.

To my family, your love and support have been my rock. Your faith in me has been a constant source of strength and inspiration.

Rev. Edward, your spiritual wisdom and encouragement have profoundly shaped this work. Thank you for your guidance and belief in this project.

Christine Lynn Jones, your insights as an educationist have been invaluable. Your dedication to nurturing young minds has greatly influenced the heart of this book.

With gratitude,

Patrick Maina.

PART I: LAYING THE FOUNDATION

CHAPTER 1: EMBRACING CHRISTIAN VALUES IN PARENTHOOD

Understanding the significance of Christian values

Parenthood is a profound and sacred journey, one that is filled with joys, challenges, and countless growth opportunities. As Christian parents, our responsibility extends beyond nurturing our children's physical and emotional well-being. It involves instilling a strong foundation of Christian values that will help and guide them throughout their lives. When we create a solid Christian basis, we may be confident that our society and nation will be safe and secure.

The Significance of Christian Values

Christian values are the moral and ethical principles rooted in the teachings of Jesus Christ. They encompass love, compassion, forgiveness, honesty, humility, etc. Embracing these values provides a moral compass that helps children make decisions aligned with their faith.

Building Character through Values

Character development is a central aspect of Christian parenting. We aim to raise children who not only believe in Christ but also live according to His teachings. Christian values form the bedrock upon which their character is built. They teach children empathy, kindness, and the importance of serving others.

Incorporating Values into Everyday Life

Instilling Christian values isn't limited to attending church on Sundays or reading the Bible occasionally. It involves incorporating these values into every facet of family life. Simple acts of love, such as showing kindness to neighbors or helping a friend in need, can be powerful lessons in Christian living.

Leading by Example

Children learn through observation. As parents, we must lead by example, demonstrating Christian values in our daily lives. Whether it's forgiving a neighbor's mistake, practicing gratitude, or being humble in our successes, our actions speak louder than words. Parents should be good role models in all aspects, including our words, actions, and behavior, as well as our dedication to Christ.

TEACHING VALUES THROUGH Stories

Biblical stories provide a rich source of teachings about Christian values. Stories like the Good Samaritan, the Prodigal Son, and the Sermon on the Mount offer valuable lessons that can be shared with children. These stories make Christian values relatable and memorable to children.

Practical Tips for Embracing Christian Values

Parents can utilize the following ways to instill Christian values in their children:

Family Devotionals: Establish regular family devotionals where you read Scripture, discuss its relevance, and pray together.

Service Opportunities: Engage in community service as a family to teach the value of helping others.

Forgiveness and Reconciliation: Encourage children to resolve conflicts peacefully and model forgiveness within the family.

Gratitude: Express gratitude for blessings and discuss the importance of recognizing God's grace in daily life.

Prayer: Teach children to pray for guidance, strength, and gratitude, emphasizing the importance of a personal relationship with God.

Attending Church: When parents attend church with their children and engage in church services, it builds a healthy Christian family.

Christian Media: Parents are encouraged to use Christian books, Christian movies, cartoons, and songs to help their children grasp the gospel. They should also aid children in memorizing Bible verses.

In Summary

- Embracing Christian values in parenthood is a foundational step in growing faith in your children.
- These values not only shape character but also provide a strong ethical framework for making choices in life.
- As parents, our role is not merely to pass on beliefs but to embody them, allowing our children to witness the transformative power of faith in action.

CHAPTER 2: NURTURING FAITH IN YOUR CHILDREN

Fostering a love for God and spirituality from a young age

As Christian parents, one of our most important responsibilities given by God is nurturing faith in our children. We seek to instill in them a love for God, a deep understanding of spirituality, and a genuine connection to their faith. The journey of nurturing faith begins from the earliest years of a child's life and continues throughout their development.

Fostering a Love for God

Nurturing faith begins with fostering a genuine love for God. This love is not merely an intellectual understanding but a heartfelt connection with our maker. Children should feel the warmth and comfort of God's love in their lives. As parents, our actions and attitudes towards God play a major role in shaping their own perception.

Practical Ways to Nurture Faith

Family Prayer: Regular family prayers provide an opportunity for children to experience a sense of community with God. Encourage children to participate by expressing their own prayers and concerns.

Bible Stories: Share age-appropriate Bible stories that captivate children's imaginations and illustrate important spiritual lessons. Discuss the stories and their relevance to daily life.

Attending Church: Regular church attendance helps children connect with their faith community, experience worship, and learn from biblical teachings.

Nature and Creation: Teach children to see God's hand in the beauty of nature. Spend time outdoors, exploring God's creation, and discussing the wonder of His works.

Faith-Based Activities: Engage in faith-based activities such as Christian arts and crafts, creating prayer journals, or participating in church events for children.

Encouraging Questions and Discussions

Children are naturally curious, and their questions about faith should be welcomed. Encourage open dialogue about God, Jesus, prayer, and other spiritual topics. When children feel that their inquiries are valued and respected, they are more likely to develop a deep and enduring faith.

The Role of Church and Sunday School/Teens Classes

Active participation in church life and Sunday School/Teens Classes can have a profound impact on a child's faith journey. It provides opportunities for them to interact with peers who share their beliefs, learn from experienced teachers, and participate in age-appropriate activities that reinforce Christian values.

Modeling Faith

Children often learn best by observing the faith of their parents. Show them what it means to have a personal relationship with God through your actions, prayers, and daily choices guided by faith. Share your personal faith journey, including periods of uncertainty and amazing connection with Jesus.

In Summary

- Nurturing faith in your children is a beautiful and ongoing journey.
- It requires patience, love, and a commitment to fostering a genuine and personal connection to God.
- As they grow, your children will carry the seeds of faith that you plant in their hearts into their own lives and the lives of future generations.

CHAPTER 3: PRAYING FOR YOUR FAMILY'S SPIRITUAL GROWTH

The power of prayer in Christian parenting

Prayer is the cornerstone of the Christian faith, and it holds a special place in the hearts of Christian parents. It is through prayer that we connect with God, seek His guidance, and invite His presence into our homes.In this chapter, we will look at the role of prayer in spiritual growth in our families, as well as how prayer can shape our Christian parenting journey.

The Power of Prayer

Prayer is more than a religious ritual; it is a direct line of communication with God. Through prayer, we express our gratitude, seek wisdom, and place our hopes and fears in God's hands. As parents, our prayers not only benefit us but also greatly impact our children's lives.

Establishing Family Prayer Rituals

One of the most meaningful ways to integrate prayer into family life is by establishing regular family prayer rituals. These rituals create a sense of unity, security, and spiritual connectedness among family members. Whether it's a morning prayer before the day begins, a mealtime prayer of thanksgiving, or bedtime prayers, these rituals instill the importance of prayer in your children's hearts.

Teaching Children to Pray

Teaching our children to pray is a vital part of their spiritual development. Begin by modeling prayer for them, showing them how to express their thoughts and feelings to God. Encourage them to use simple, heartfelt language when they pray. Emphasize that prayer is not about perfection but about sincere communication with God.

Praying for Your Children's Needs

As parents, we naturally want the best for our children. Through prayer, we can bring our concerns and hopes for them to God. Pray for their safety, health, academic success, and spiritual growth. Trust that God hears your prayers and petiton is working behind the scenes in their lives in ways that you may not always see.

Praying as a Family

In addition to individual and mealtime prayers, praying together as a family has a unique significance. Family prayers allow everyone to share their intentions, joys, and concerns. It strengthens the family bond and reinforces the idea that faith is not just an individual pursuit but a shared journey.

Praying in Challenging Times

Life is filled with challenges, and as parents, we may face difficult moments in our family's journey. During these times, turn to prayer for guidance, strength, and solace. Share your struggles with God and trust in His wisdom to navigate the challenges that come your way.

Praying for Your Family's Spiritual Growth

Ultimately, our prayers should center on our family's spiritual growth. Pray for a deepening of faith, a greater understanding of God's love, and a commitment to living out Christian values. Pray that your family's faith journey may be a source of inspiration and hope to others.

<u>In Summary</u>

- Prayer is a powerful tool in Christian parenting, allowing us to invite God's presence into our homes and guide our family's spiritual growth.
- As you embrace prayer as a central practice in your family, remember that it is a journey.
- The conversations you have with God and the lessons you teach your children through prayer are seeds that continue to

grow and flourish in the years to come.

CHAPTER 4: BUILDING A CHRIST-CENTERED HOME

Creating a home environment that reflects Christian values
The home is where faith is lived out daily, and as Christian parents, we have an important task of creating a Christ-centered environment for our families. Building a Christ-centered home involves infusing every aspect of family life with the love, teachings, and values of Jesus Christ.

The Importance of a Christ-Centered Home

A Christ-centered home serves as a sanctuary where faith is nurtured and lived out authentically. It is a place where children witness the love of Christ through their parents' actions, where prayer is a natural part of daily life, and where Christian values guide decisions and interactions.

Incorporating Christian Symbols

Christian symbols and artifacts can serve as powerful reminders of faith within the home. Displaying a cross or crucifix, placing a Bible verse, or having Christian artwork can visually reinforce the family's commitment to Christ. Hanging Bible scriptures with pictures on their bedroom walls will help children grasp the Bible better.

Family Devotional Time

Establishing a routine of family devotional time is a cornerstone of a Christ-centered home. Gather as a family to read Scripture, discuss its relevance to daily life, and engage in prayer together. Family devotionals foster spiritual growth and provide an opportunity for open dialogue about faith.

Service to Others

A Christ-centered home is one that places a strong emphasis on serving others. Engage in acts of kindness and service as a family. Whether it's volunteering together, helping a neighbor in need, or participating in community outreach, these actions reflect the love of Christ in action.

Practicing Forgiveness

Forgiveness is central to the Christian faith. Teach your children the importance of forgiveness through your own actions and by encouraging them to forgive others. Model forgiveness within the family, emphasizing reconciliation and love.

Blessing and Prayer

Incorporate blessings and prayers into your family daily routines. Bless your children before they go to bed, and pray for guidance, protection, and gratitude as a family. These moments of prayer create a sense of spiritual connection and security.

Meals with Meaning

Mealtime can be an opportunity for spiritual nourishment. Begin or end family meals with prayer, and use this time to discuss the day's events and express gratitude for God's provision.

Creating a Peaceful Atmosphere

As a parent strive to create a peaceful and loving atmosphere within your home. Encourage harmony and respect among family members, and address conflicts with patience and empathy. A Christ-centered home is one where the fruits tof the Spirit—love, joy, peace, patience, kindness, goodness, faithfulness, gentleness, and self-control—are evident.

Holidays and Traditions

Christian holidays and traditions play a significant role in building a Christ-centered home. Celebrate holidays like Christmas and Easter with a focus on their spiritual significance. Create family traditions that reinforce Christian values and bring joy to your home.

<u>IN SUMMARY</u>

- Building a Christ-centered home is a continuous journey that requires intentionality and commitment.
- It is a place where faith is not confined to a single room or moment but permeates every aspect of family life.
- As you create this environment, remember that your home is a reflection of your faith, and it serves as a powerful witness to your children and all who enter its doors.

PART II: SHAPING CHARACTER AND VIRTUE

CHAPTER 5: TEACHING CHRISTIAN VALUES AND VIRTUES

Instilling the principles of Christ-like living

As Christian parents, one of our central roles is to impart Christian values and virtues to our children. These values and virtues reflect the teachings of Jesus Christ and guide us in living a life that aligns with His example. In this chapter, we will explore how to effectively teach and instill these principles in your children's lives.

Understanding Christian Values and Virtues

Christian values and virtues encompass a range of qualities that reflect the teachings of Jesus. These include love, compassion, humility, honesty, forgiveness, gratitude, kindness, and many more. Understanding the significance of these values is essential before we can impart them to our children.

Modeling Christ-Like Behavior

Children learn by example, and as parents, we must model Christ-like behavior in our daily lives. Our actions speak louder than words, and when children witness us living out these values, they are more likely to adopt them as their own. Show love and compassion to others, practice forgiveness, and be humble in your successes.

Teaching Through Stories and Parables

The Bible is a rich source of parables and stories that illustrate Christian values and virtues. Share these stories with your children and discuss the lessons they convey. For example, the parable of the Good Samaritan teaches the value of compassion and helping others in need.

Practical Application

Christian values are not merely theoretical ideas; they should be integrated into everyday life. Encourage your children to practice kindness, gratitude, and forgiveness in their interactions with family, friends, and others. Teach them to see the needs of those less fortunate and how they can help.

Open and Age-Appropriate Discussions

Engage in open and age-appropriate discussions about Christian values and virtues. Encourage your children to ask questions and express their thoughts and feelings. Discuss real-life situations where these values can be applied and the positive impact they have on individuals and communities.

Prayer for Guidance

Pray with your children for guidance in living out Christian values. Ask for God's help in understanding and practicing these principles. Prayer provides a spiritual foundation and reinforces the importance of seeking divine assistance in daily life.

Celebrating Your Child's Good Deeds

Celebrate and acknowledge good deeds and behaviors in your children. When they display kindness, honesty, or generosity, praise them for their efforts. Reinforce the idea that living by Christian values brings joy and blessings.

Consistency and Patience

Teaching Christian values and virtues is a lifelong journey. Be consistent in your efforts, and have patience as your children grow and develop. Understand that they may make mistakes, but these moments provide opportunities for growth and learning.

<u>**In summary**</u>

- Teaching Christian values and virtues to your children is a sacred duty that shapes their character and guides them in living a life rooted in faith.
- As you embark on this journey, remember that your role as a parent is not only to impart knowledge but also to nurture the heart of the children.
- By modeling Christ-like behavior, engaging in open discussions, and celebrating virtuous actions, you are laying a strong foundation for your children's spiritual growth.

CHAPTER 6: DISCIPLINE WITH LOVE AND FAITH

Nurturing Christian character through loving guidance
Discipline is an important aspect of parenting, but it takes on a unique dimension in Christian parenting. We are called to discipline our children with love, wisdom, and faith, guiding them toward a deeper understanding of Christian values and virtues. In this chapter, we explore the principles of discipline within a Christian set-up.

Understanding Christian Discipline

Christian discipline is rooted in love and seeks to shape a child's character while nurturing their faith. It is not about punishment but about teaching right from wrong, instilling values, and fostering spiritual growth. Discipline in a Christian home is guided by the teachings of Jesus Christ.

Love as the Foundation

Love is at the heart of Christian discipline. It is through love that we correct, guide, and train our children. Emphasize to your children that discipline is an expression of your love for them and your desire for their well-being. They should never doubt your unconditional love, even in moments of correction.

Consistency and Clear Expectations

Consistency is key in discipline. Set clear expectations, goals and boundaries for your children, and ensure that consequences for actions are consistent. This consistency provides a sense of security and helps children understand the consequences of their choices.

Teaching Repentance and Forgiveness

Christian discipline teaches the importance of repentance and forgiveness. When children make mistakes, guide them to acknowledge their actions, seek forgiveness from God, and make amends with those they may have harmed. Reinforce the idea that God's love and forgiveness are always available.

Discipline with Words and Actions

Discipline should primarily involve words and actions that express your disappointment or concern. Avoid harsh physical discipline and instead focus on communication and guidance. Teach your children to understand the consequences of their actions and the impact on others. **Proverbs 23:13-14** reminds us that we should not withhold the rod from our children. This is a noble task, but we must perform it with Godly wisdom.

TEACHING RESPONSIBILITY and Accountability

Christian discipline also emphasizes personal responsibility and accountability. Encourage your children to take ownership of their actions and decisions. This helps them mature and grow in their understanding of right and wrong.

Restoration and Healing

After discipline, focus on restoration and healing. Reassure your children of your love, and use these moments as opportunities to teach and guide them toward better choices. Show them that mistakes can be valuable lessons on the path of Christian growth.

Seeking God's Guidance

Prayer plays a vital role in Christian discipline. Seek God's guidance in your approach to discipline, asking for wisdom, patience, and discernment. Pray for your children, that they may understand the lessons being taught and grow in their faith.

The Role of Grace

Christian discipline recognizes the importance of grace. As God extends His grace to us, we too should extend grace to our children. Understand that they are not perfect and that mistakes are part of their learning journey. Show grace, forgiveness, and love consistently.

<u>**In summary**</u>

- Discipline with love and faith is an integral part of Christian parenting.
- It is an opportunity to shape your children's character, instill Christian values, and guide them toward a deeper relationship with God.
- As you discipline, remember that your actions and words should reflect the teachings of Jesus, who embodied love, forgiveness, and grace.

CHAPTER 7: PARENTING TEENS WITH CHRISTIAN PRINCIPLES

Guiding adolescents through the challenges of faith and identity The teenage years are a period characterized by significant transformation and self-discovery. As Christian parents, it's crucial to navigate this transitional phase with wisdom, patience, and a strong foundation of Christian principles. In this chapter, we will look at the unique challenges of parenting teenagers within a Christian context.

Understanding the Teenage Journey

Adolescence is a time of change, both physically and emotionally. Teens are searching for their identity and independence while facing peer pressure, academic challenges, and societal influences. Teens have mood swings, and it is important to understand them. It's essential to understand and encourage them through their struggles.

Maintaining Open Communication

Open and honest communication is paramount when parenting teenagers. Create an environment where your teens feel comfortable discussing their thoughts, feelings, and questions about faith and life. Be a listening ear and provide guidance rooted in Christian values.

Consistent Prayer

Prayer becomes even more crucial during the teenage years. Continue to pray for your teenagers, asking for God's guidance, protection, and wisdom as they navigate challenges. Encourage them to develop their prayer life and seek God's direction in their decisions.

Setting Boundaries

Establish clear boundaries while allowing room for independence. Boundaries should reflect Christian values and safety concerns. Discuss the reasons behind rules and boundaries, emphasizing how they align with your faith and love for them.

Teaching Critical Thinking

Encourage critical thinking and discernment in your teenagers. Teach them to evaluate information, media, and peer influences in light of Christian principles. Equip them to make informed decisions that align with their faith.

MODELING FAITH

Your teenagers are watching your example closely. Model a genuine and active faith by attending church together, participating in spiritual activities, and demonstrating Christian values in your daily life. You should be sincere, and this will have a lasting impact to the teens.

Addressing Challenges with Grace

Teenagers may make mistakes or face challenges that test their faith. Approach these moments with grace, emphasizing that God's love and forgiveness are always available. Provide guidance and support as they learn and grow.

Encouraging Service and Compassion

Foster a sense of service and compassion in your teenagers. Engage in volunteer activities or mission work as a family, demonstrating the importance of helping others in need. These experiences can deepen their faith and understanding of Christ's teachings. It will also keep them busy thus channeling their energy in a positive way.

NAVIGATING PEER PRESSURE

Discuss the concept of peer pressure with your teenagers. Teach them to make choices based on their faith and values, even when faced with pressure from their friends. Encourage them to seek friendships with like-minded individuals who share their faith.

Preparing for the Future

As teenagers approach adulthood, help them prepare for the future with faith in mind. Discuss vocational choices, career, relationships, and life goals in the context of Christian values. Provide guidance on making decisions that align with their faith.

Teach Emotional Intelligence

Acknowledge your teen's emotions. Let them know that it's okay to feel upset or angry at times. Making them feel heard and understood is a very good way to show you care. Help your teen understand their emotions and how to manage them. Teach them techniques like Bible reading, deep breathing, mindfulness, or journaling to express their feelings in a healthy way.

<u>**In summary**</u>

- Parenting teenagers with Christian principles is a challenging yet rewarding journey.
- By understanding their unique struggles, you can help your teenagers navigate this transformative phase while deepening their relationship with God.
- By being there for them and walking the journey of adolescent stage with them will make the teens make the right decisions.

CHAPTER 8: FOSTERING SIBLING BONDS THROUGH FAITH

Nurturing strong sibling relationships grounded in Christian values

Sibling relationships are among the most enduring bonds in a person's life. As Christian parents, you have the opportunity to cultivate these relationships in ways that reflect your faith and values. This chapter will explore the importance of fostering sibling bonds through faith.

The Significance of Sibling Bonds

Siblings share a unique and lifelong connection. They are companions on the journey of life, offering each other support, understanding, and companionship. As parents, you play a vital role in helping your children build strong, loving relationships with their siblings which will transit to their adulthood.

Modeling Christian Values

One of the most effective ways to foster sibling bonds through faith is by modeling Christian values in your interactions with your children. Demonstrate love, kindness, forgiveness, and compassion in your relationships with them. Show them what it means to follow Christ's example in their interactions with each other.

Teaching Conflict Resolution

Conflict is a natural part of sibling relationships. Use these moments as teaching opportunities to the children. Encourage your children to resolve conflicts through dialogue, understanding, and forgiveness. Teach them the importance of seeking reconciliation, just as Christ calls us to do.

Shared Worship and Prayer

Include siblings in your family's worship and prayer routines. When they come together to worship and pray, it strengthens their sense of unity and shared faith. Encourage them to pray for each other's well-being and spiritual growth.

Sibling Bible Studies

Organize sibling Bible studies or discussions where they can explore Scripture together. This deepens their understanding of God's Word and creates a bonding experience as they share their insights and questions.

Encouraging Acts of Kindness

Challenge your children to perform acts of kindness for their siblings. These acts can be as simple as helping with chores, offering a kind word, or providing support during challenging times. By doing so, they practice the values of selflessness and love.

Building Each Other Up

Teach your children the importance of building each other up. Encourage them to offer words of encouragement, appreciation, and affirmation. This fosters a sense of security and belonging within the sibling relationship.

Celebrating Each Other's Gifts

Every child is uniquely gifted by God. Celebrate and affirm each child's talents and abilities. Encourage siblings to support and celebrate each other's successes, fostering a spirit of cooperation rather than competition.

Creating Shared Family Traditions

Establish family traditions that involve all siblings. These traditions could be related to holidays, special family outings, or volunteering together. Shared experiences create lasting memories and strengthen bonds.

PRAYING FOR SIBLING Unity

Include prayers for sibling unity in your family's prayer time. Ask God to bless their relationships, help them grow in love and understanding, and to always draw them closer to Him through their bonds with each other.

Avoid Comparison

Avoid comparing your children to one another. Each child has their unique strengths and challenges, and comparing them can lead to resentment. Treat each child equally by giving gifts or other items equally and spending quality time with each child.

Fair Discipline

Apply consistent rules and consequences for all children. Ensure that discipline is fair and appropriate for each child's age and behavior.

<u>In summary</u>

- Fostering sibling bonds through faith is a vital aspect of Christian parenting.
- By exhibiting Christian principles, you can assist your children in developing close, loving relationships with their siblings that they can carry into adulthood.
- As a parent you have a duty to create a loving and supportive environment for your children.

PART III: OVERCOMING CHALLENGES

CHAPTER 9: NAVIGATING CHALLENGES WITH FAITHFUL PARENTING

Drawing on faith to overcome obstacles in Christian parenting
Christian parenting is a journey filled with joys and challenges. While faith provides a strong foundation, there will be times when you face difficult situations that require unwavering trust in God's guidance. In this chapter, we will explore how to navigate challenges with faithful parenting.

Recognizing Life's Trials

Life is filled with trials, and as parents, you may encounter various challenges, both expected and unexpected. These challenges can include financial struggles, health issues, conflicts within the family, or external pressures that impact your children.

Turning to Prayer

When challenges arise, turn to prayer as your first response. Seek God's guidance, wisdom, and strength in your moments of uncertainty. Pray for clarity, patience, and the faith to endure. Know that God is always listening and ready to provide comfort and guidance.

Maintaining Open Communication

Encourage open communication within your family. When challenges arise, create a safe space for your children to express their feelings, concerns, and questions without fear. Listening with empathy and understanding fosters a sense of security and trust.

Modeling Resilience

Your children are observing how you respond to challenges. Model resilience by demonstrating how to face difficulties with faith and courage. Show them that setbacks can be opportunities for growth and learning.

Seeking Support from Your Fellow Faith Community

Lean on your fellow faith community for support. Share your challenges with fellow parents and seek advice and encouragement. Your church family can provide a valuable support system during difficult times.

Teaching Trust in God

Use challenging moments as opportunities to teach your children to trust in God. Share stories from Scripture where characters faced adversity and overcame it through faith. Remind your children that God is always with them.

Staying Focused on Your Values

During challenging times, it's easy to lose sight of your values. Reaffirm your commitment to Christian principles and values in your family life. Let your faith guide your decisions and actions.

Finding Strength in Scripture

Turn to Scripture for strength and inspiration. There are numerous passages that offer comfort and encouragement during challenging moments. Memorize and reflect on these verses as a family.

Supporting Each Other

As a family, support each other through challenges. Encourage teamwork, empathy, and mutual assistance. Let your children witness the power of love and unity in overcoming obstacles.

Seeking Professional Help When Needed

In some situations, it may be necessary to seek professional help. Don't hesitate to consult counselors, therapists, or other experts who can provide guidance and support tailored to your family's needs.

IN SUMMARY

- Navigating challenges with faithful parenting requires trust in God's guidance.
- As you continue your journey of Christian parenting, remember that challenges are an inevitable part of life, but with faith, love, and God's guidance, you can overcome them

CHAPTER 10: PARENTING IN A DIGITAL AGE WITH CHRISTIAN VALUES

Navigating the challenges and opportunities of the digital era
In today's world, technology and the digital age play a significant role in the lives of our children. As Christian parents, it is our responsibility to guide our children through the digital landscape while instilling Christian values. In this chapter, we will explore how to parent in a digital age with Christian values.

The Digital Landscape

Technology has transformed the way we live, work, and communicate. Children are growing up in a world where smartphones, social media, and online content are a daily part of life. It is essential to understand this landscape to effectively guide our children.

Setting Healthy Boundaries

One of the first steps in parenting in a digital age is setting healthy boundaries. Establish rules for screen time, online content, and social media usage. These boundaries should be age-appropriate and aligned with your Christian values.

MODELING DIGITAL DISCERNMENT

Children learn by example, so model digital discernment in your own technology use. Show them how to use technology responsibly, avoid harmful content, and prioritize face-to-face interactions.

Open Communication

Foster open communication with your children about their online experiences. Encourage them to share their experience, questions, concerns, or encounters with anything that contradicts your Christian values. Be a non-judgmental and understanding listener.

Teaching Digital Literacy

Educate your children about digital literacy and critical thinking. Help them differentiate between reliable and unreliable online sources. Teach them to be mindful of the information they encounter and to question what they see.

Online Safety and Privacy

Discuss online safety and privacy with your children. Teach them about the potential risks and dangers of sharing personal information online. Ensure they understand the importance of privacy settings and safe online behavior. Educate your children about cyber bullying and other children harassers who try to entice them.

Balancing Digital and Offline Activities

Encourage a balance between digital and physical activities. Emphasize the importance of spending quality time with family, engaging in physical activities, and nurturing face-to-face relationships.

Choosing Positive Content

Guide your children in choosing positive and uplifting online content. Help them find websites, apps, and media that align with your Christian values and promote wholesome entertainment and learning.

Online Ministry and Outreach

Explore online ministry and outreach opportunities with your children. Encourage them to use technology to spread the message of faith, connect with Christian communities, and engage in acts of kindness and service online.

Prayer and Reflection

Integrate prayer and reflection into your family's digital experience. Encourage your children to pray about their online interactions, seek God's guidance in digital choices, and reflect on how their online behavior aligns with Christian values.

<u>In summary</u>

- It is your responsibility as a parent to teach your kids Christian values as they navigate the digital world.
- As Christian parents, you have the opportunity to guide your children through the digital landscape with wisdom, discernment, and faith.
- By instilling Christian values in their digital interactions, you help them navigate the challenges and opportunities of the digital age while staying true to their faith.

CHAPTER 11: BALANCING FAMILY, CHURCH, COMMUNITY AND WORK

Finding harmony in the midst of life's demands

As Christian parents, you often find yourselves juggling multiple responsibilities—raising your children, nurturing your faith, social activities and fulfilling work commitments. Finding balance among these demands can be challenging, but it is important for maintaining a strong Christian family. In this chapter, we will explore strategies for balancing family, faith, social activities and work while upholding Christian values.

The Juggling Act

Balancing family, faith, social activities and work can sometimes feel like a juggling act. The demands of your career, your commitment to your Christian faith, and your responsibilities as parents may seem overwhelming. However, with faith as your foundation, you can find harmony in these areas.

Prioritizing Family and Faith

Begin by prioritizing your family and faith. Dedicate time to nurture your relationship with God through prayer, worship, and studying Scripture. Make family time a priority, ensuring that you allocate moments for quality interactions with your spouse and children.

Effective Time Management

Effective time management is crucial. Organize your schedule to allocate time for work, family, and faith-related activities. Create a balanced routine that allows for both individual and family devotionals, worship services, and quality family time.

Setting Boundaries

Establish clear boundaries between work and family life. When you're with your family, be fully present, and avoid bringing work-related stress or distractions into your home. Similarly, when you're at work, focus on your responsibilities and avoid unnecessary distractions.

Incorporating Faith into Daily Life

Integrate your faith into your daily life. Make faith a central part of your family's routine, whether it's praying together before meals, discussing Bible stories before bedtime, or volunteering as a family for community service.

Seeking Support

Lean on your church community for support and encouragement. Share your challenges and seek guidance from fellow believers who may have faced similar struggles. Your church family can provide valuable insights and a network of support.

Family Work-Life Balance

Include your children in discussions about work-life balance. Explain to them the importance of your work, the significance of your faith, and the need for quality family time. Encourage them to share their inner feelings and concerns about your schedule.

Flexibility and Adaptability

Recognize that life can be unpredictable, and sometimes adjustments are necessary. Be flexible and adaptable in your approach to balancing family, faith, social life and work. Embrace change as an opportunity for growth.

Stress Management

Stress is a natural part of life, but it's essential to manage it effectively. Turn to prayer, meditation, or relaxation techniques to alleviate stress. It is best to avoid transferring your work-related stress on your family. If you're having trouble coping with work-related stress, consider seeking advice and assistance from a counselor or therapist.

Self-Care and Rest

Remember to prioritize self-care and rest. A well-rested and spiritually nourished parent is better equipped to meet the demands of work and family life. Prioritize getting adequate sleep, eating healthily, and exercising regularly.

<u>In summary</u>

- Balancing family, faith, and work is a continuous journey that requires intentional effort.
- Prioritizing family and faith and incorporating all members of the family will help you find peace in the face of life's pressures.

PART IV: GROWING IN FAITH

CHAPTER 12: RAISING COMPASSIONATE AND SERVICE-ORIENTED CHILDREN

Cultivating a heart for others in Christian parenting
As Christian parents, one of our most significant responsibilities is to instill in our children a sense of compassion and a heart for service. Teaching them to love and care for others is a fundamental aspect of Christian parenting. In this chapter, we will explore how to raise compassionate and service-oriented children.

The Call to Compassion

Christianity calls us to love our neighbors as ourselves, to show kindness and compassion to those in need. Instilling this value in your children is an essential part of their spiritual growth.

Leading by Example

Children learn by example, so it's crucial to model compassion and service in your own life. Engage in acts of kindness, volunteer as a family, and demonstrate empathy toward those less fortunate

Teaching Empathy

Empathy is the foundation of compassion. Encourage your children to see the world through the eyes of others. Discuss the feelings and needs of those who are suffering or in challenging situations.

Acts of Kindness

Encourage your children to carry out acts of kindness regularly. These acts can be as simple as helping a neighbor, donating to a charity, or comforting a friend in need. Teach them that even small actions can make a significant impact.

Community Involvement

Get involved in community service as a family. Participate in local charity events, volunteer at shelters/homes, or engage in initiatives that support the less fortunate. This hands-on experience will deepen your children's understanding of compassion.

Scripture and Compassion

Explore Scripture with your children to illustrate the importance of compassion and service. Share stories of Jesus's teachings and actions that exemplify love and kindness towards others.

Prayer for Others

Incorporate prayers for others into your family's routine. Encourage your children to pray for those in need, both locally and globally. Teach them that prayer is a powerful way to express compassion and seek God's help for those who are suffering.

Cultivating a Giving Spirit

Help your children develop a giving spirit by involving them in decisions about charitable giving. Allow them to donate a percentage of their savings or items to a cause they are passionate about, instilling a sense of responsibility for others.

Empowering Acts of Service

As your children grow, empower them to take the initiative in acts of service. Encourage them to identify needs in their school, church, or community and brainstorm ways to address them.

Reflecting on the Impact

Regularly discuss the impact of your family's compassionate actions. Share stories of how your acts of kindness have made a difference in the lives of others. This reflection reinforces the value of compassion.

IN SUMMARY

- Raising compassionate and service-oriented children is a vital aspect of Christian parenting which will make the world a better place to live in.
- You will cultivate in your children a compassion for others by setting an example of generosity with your resources and possessions.
- One of the most important aspects of Christian parenting is teaching your kids to love and care for other people.

CHAPTER 13: ENCOURAGING A LOVE FOR SCRIPTURE AND PRAYER

Nurturing spiritual growth through the Word and communion with God

In Christian parenting, nurturing a love for Scripture and prayer in your children is paramount. These practices form the foundation of a deep and meaningful relationship with God. In this chapter, we will explore how to encourage a love for Scripture and prayer in your children.

The Power of Scripture and Prayer

Scripture is God's word, and prayer is our direct communication with Him. Together, they serve as essential tools for spiritual growth and understanding of God's will.

Leading by Example

Children learn by example. Demonstrate your own love for Scripture by engaging in regular Bible reading and study. Likewise, model the importance of prayer in your daily life. Your children will be more likely to follow your lead.

AGE-APPROPRIATE BIBLE Engagement

Select age-appropriate versions of the Bible for your children. Share Bible stories with them and gradually introduce them to Scripture.

Consider using children's Bibles or Bible storybooks to make the content more accessible.

Family Bible Study

Hold family Bible study sessions where you read and discuss Scripture together. Encourage your children to ask questions and express themselves without fear. This fosters a sense of community and spiritual growth.

Praying Together

Incorporate family prayer time into your daily routine. Create a dedicated space for prayer and involve your children in these moments of communion with God. Encourage them to share their own prayers and concerns.

Prayer for Guidance

Teach your children to seek God's guidance through prayer. Encourage them to pray about decisions, challenges, and opportunities in their lives. Help them understand that God is a source of wisdom and comfort.

MEMORIZING SCRIPTURE

Introduce Scripture memorization to your children. Select key verses or passages that align with Christian values and have them learn and recite these verses. It's a powerful way to internalize God's word.

Storytelling from Scripture

Share Bible stories with your children beyond just reading. Tell these stories in a way that captivates their imagination and highlights the moral and spiritual lessons within them.

Prayer Journaling

Introduce the concept of prayer journaling to older children. Encourage them to keep a journal where they write down their prayers, thoughts, and reflections on Scripture. This practice helps deepen their connection with God.

Church Community Worship

Attend church services and community worship as a family. These experiences can reinforce the importance of Scripture and prayer in the Christian faith and provide opportunities for spiritual growth.

Reflecting on God's Word

Regularly discuss the lessons learned from Scripture with your children. Encourage them to think about how these teachings apply to their daily lives and how they can live out Christian values.

In Summary

- Encouraging a love for Scripture and prayer is a vital aspect of Christian parenting.
- Reflecting on God's word will help your children grow spiritually and develop a deep and meaningful connection with God.

CHAPTER 14: THE ROLE OF WORSHIP AND CHURCH IN FAMILY LIFE

Strengthening faith through communal worship and fellowship

In Christian parenting, the role of worship and church in family life is foundational. Attending church services, engaging in communal worship, and participating in the life of the church community can greatly enhance the spiritual growth of your family.In this chapter, we will look at the role of worship and church in family life.

The Importance of Worship

Worship is an essential component of Christian faith. It is a time for believers to come together to praise and connect with God. Encouraging your family to engage in regular worship serves several essential purposes:

Communion with God

Worship allows your family to commune with God as a collective unit. It's a time to express gratitude, seek guidance, and deepen your relationship with Him.

Church Community Building

Attending church services and worshiping with other believers fosters a sense of community. Your family becomes part of a larger spiritual family, providing support and fellowship.

Spiritual Education

Church services often include teachings, sermons, and discussions that help educate your family about the Christian faith. This enhances your understanding of Scripture and Christian values.

Family Participation

Involve your family in the worship experience. Encourage children to participate in church activities, such as Sunday school, Teens classes, youth groups, or music ministries. These experiences can deepen their connection to the church community.

Regular Church Attendance

Make regular church attendance a priority. Establish a routine that includes Sunday worship services and other church-related activities. Consistency in attendance strengthens your family's faith.

Worship at Home

While attending church is crucial, worship can also take place within your home. Hold family devotional times where you read Scripture, pray together, and sing hymns or worship songs.

Participating in Church Life

Engage in the life of your church beyond Sunday services. Participate in church events, volunteer for church community service projects, and attend church gatherings. This involvement deepens your connection to the church community.

Spiritual Mentorship

Seek spiritual mentorship for your children within the church community. Encourage them to form relationships with adults who can provide guidance and support in their faith journey.

Family Reflection

After church services or family devotions, engage in discussions about the lessons learned and how they apply to your family's daily life. Reflect on how the teachings and worship experiences strengthen your faith.

Supporting One Another

Use the church community as a support system. Share your family's challenges and joys with fellow church members. Seek guidance and prayer when needed, and offer support to others in return.

IN SUMMARY

- The role of worship and church in family life is integral to Christian parenting.
- As a parent, you have a responsibility to show your family where to worship, which will help your children grow spiritually.
- Your family's spiritual growth can be greatly helped by attending church services, participating in group worship, and being involved in the church activities.

CHAPTER 15: PASSING DOWN GENERATIONAL WISDOM

Preserving and sharing the Christian faith across generations
As Christian parents, one of your most significant responsibilities is passing down generational wisdom rooted in the Christian faith. This wisdom forms the foundation for your children's spiritual growth and their ability to carry the torch of faith forward. In this chapter, we will explore the importance of passing down generational wisdom.

The Value of Generational Wisdom

Generational wisdom encompasses the teachings, values, and experiences passed down from one generation to the next. In the context of Christian parenting, it refers to the rich heritage of faith and spiritual insight that has been cultivated in your family over the years.

Family Traditions

Incorporate family traditions into your Christian parenting. These traditions can include celebrating religious holidays, family prayers, reading from the same Bible that has been passed down through generations, and sharing stories of faith of old generation.

Shared Stories

Share stories of faith from your family's history. These stories can include moments of spiritual growth, answered prayers, and instances where God's guidance and presence were evident. Personal narratives create a strong connection to the Christian faith.

Teaching Through Experience

Encourage your children to learn from your experiences and the experiences of older family members. Share how faith has played a role in navigating challenges and making important life decisions.

Family Devotionals

Incorporate family devotionals into your routine. These sessions provide opportunities to read Scripture, discuss its relevance to your lives, and share insights. They also create an environment for open dialogue about faith.

Spiritual Mentorship

Encourage your children to seek mentorship from older, wiser believers within the church community. Connecting with individuals who have a strong foundation in the faith can provide invaluable guidance and support.

Passing Down Family Bibles

If your family has a treasured family Bible, consider passing it down to the next generation. This symbolizes the continuity of faith and the importance of God's word in your family's history.

Retelling Family Testimonies

Regularly retell family testimonies of God's faithfulness. Remind your children of times when God answered prayers, provided in times of need, and guided your family's path.

Reflecting on Ancestral Faith

Encourage your children to reflect on the faith of their ancestors. Help them appreciate the sacrifices and dedication of those who came before them, laying the groundwork for their own faith journey.

Living a Legacy of Faith

Demonstrate the practical aspects of living a life of faith. Show how faith informs your decisions, relationships, and values. Be a living example of the generational wisdom you wish to impart.

IN SUMMARY

- Passing down generational wisdom is a sacred duty in Christian parenting.
- As a parent, you ensure that the Christian faith continues and endures across generations.
- Christian parenting ensures that your family's legacy is carried forward by setting and providing the appropriate direction for your family's path, ensuring that God remains the center of the family.

CHAPTER 16: EMBRACING ETERNITY WITH FAITH

reparing your family for an eternal perspective

As Christian parents, your journey is not just about the present but also about preparing your family for an eternity with God. This final chapter explores the concept of embracing eternity with faith, ensuring that your family's perspective goes beyond the temporal to the eternal.

The Eternal Perspective

The Christian faith is built on the belief in eternal life with God. It's essential to help your family understand that this earthly life is just a part of the larger, eternal journey.

Teaching about Heaven

Discuss heaven with your children. Explain the concept of eternal life with God and the hope it brings. Share passages from Scripture that describe the beauty and joy of heaven.

Facing Mortality with Faith

As part of embracing eternity, address the topic of mortality with your family. Teach them that death is not the end but a transition to eternal life for believers. This perspective can provide comfort during times of loss.

Living with Purpose

Help your children understand that their earthly lives have a purpose in the grander scheme of eternity. Encourage them to use their time on earth to serve God, love others, and make a positive impact.

Teaching about Judgment

Discuss the Biblical concept of judgment. Emphasize the importance of living a life aligned with Christian values, knowing that our actions will be weighed in the balance.

Embracing Hope

In times of difficulty and uncertainty, remind your family of the hope that faith brings. Trust that God's promises of eternal life and His presence will sustain you through life's challenges.

Preparing for Eternity

Guide your children in their personal relationship with God. Encourage daily prayer, Bible reading, and living out Christian values. These practices prepare them for eternity and bring them closer to God.

Supporting Each Other

Create an environment where your family supports each other's faith journey. Pray for one another, discuss spiritual matters, and provide a safe space for questions and doubts.

Worship with an Eternal Perspective

During worship and church activities, emphasize the eternal nature of your faith. Help your family connect their earthly worship with the anticipation of worshiping God for all eternity.

Living in Gratitude

Instill a sense of gratitude in your family for the gift of eternal life through Christ. Encourage thankfulness for the hope and assurance of spending eternity with God.

<u>In Summary</u>

- Embracing eternity with faith is the culmination of your Christian parenting journey.
- By teaching about heaven, you equip your family to see beyond the temporal and embrace the eternal.
- As you conclude this journey, may your family continue to grow in faith, hope, and love, cherishing the gift of eternal life with God.

PART V: SPECIAL CIRCUMSTANCES AND RELATIONSHIPS

CHAPTER 17: PARENTING SPECIAL NEEDS CHILDREN WITH GRACE

Navigating the unique challenges of special needs parenting
While every child is a gift from God, parenting a child with special needs presents unique challenges and blessings. In this chapter, we will explore the importance of parenting special needs children with grace and love.

Understanding Special Needs

Before diving into the challenges and rewards of special needs parenting, it's crucial to understand what "special needs" means. Special needs children may have physical, intellectual, or emotional differences that require extra care, support, and attention.

Unconditional Love

The foundation of parenting special needs children is unconditional love. Embrace your child as they are, recognizing their inherent worth and the special gifts they bring into your family.

Seeking Support

Connect with support networks within your church and community. Seek guidance from parents who have walked similar paths and learn from their experiences.

Patience and Flexibility

Special needs parenting demands patience and flexibility. Be prepared for unexpected developments and setbacks, and approach them with a calm and understanding heart.

Advocacy

Become an advocate for your child within the church community and educational system. Ensure that they receive the support and accommodations they need to thrive.

Inclusion in Church Life

Work with your church to create an inclusive environment where your special needs child can actively participate in church activities and worship.

Spiritual Growth

Recognize that parenting a special needs child can deepen your faith. It can be an opportunity to witness God's grace in unexpected ways and grow spiritually as a family.

Respite and Self-Care

Taking care of yourself is crucial. Seek respite care to ensure you have time for self-care and rejuvenation.

Community Involvement

Engage your special needs child in church and community activities and events, fostering social connections and a sense of belonging.

Celebrating Achievements

Celebrate your child's achievements, no matter how small they may seem. These milestones are significant and represent your child's growth and progress.

Sibling Support

Offer support to your other children, as they may also face unique challenges and emotions related to having a special needs sibling. Let every member of your family show love to the children with special needs.

Embracing Grace

Remember that parenting special needs children is a journey of grace. Embrace the challenges and joys, relying on God's grace to guide you.

In Summary

- Parenting special needs children with grace is a testament to the power of love, faith, and resilience.
- Understanding that special needs children are a blessing will need you to create an environment in which your special needs child feels warm and loved.
- As your journey in Christian parenting unfolds, may you continue to experience God's boundless love and grace, guiding you through every step of this extraordinary path.

CHAPTER 18: STRENGTHENING MARITAL BONDS IN CHRISTIAN PARENTING

Nurturing your marriage amidst the joys and challenges of parenthood

Marriage is a sacred union ordained by God, and it plays a central role in Christian parenting. Strong marital relationships provide a safe and secure atmosphere for your children to grow up in. This chapter explores the importance of strengthening marital bonds as you navigate the joys and challenges of parenthood together.

Prioritizing Your Marriage

Parenthood can be all-consuming, but it's essential to remember that your marriage came first. Continue to prioritize your spouse and your relationship amidst the demands of parenting.

Open Communication

A healthy marriage is built on effective communication. Keep the lines of communication open, discussing your needs, dreams, and concerns with one another.

Quality Time Together

Allocate quality time for just the two of you. Date nights, weekend getaways, or even quiet evenings at home can help you stay connected as a couple.

Supporting Each Other

Parenting is a team effort. Support each other in your roles as parents and partners. Encourage and affirm one another's contributions to the family.

Shared Spiritual Growth

Nurture your spiritual growth together. Pray as a couple, read Scripture, and attend church services together. Your faith journey should be intertwined, deepening your bond with each other and with God.

Navigating Parenthood as a Team

Make parenting decisions together. Discuss discipline strategies, educational choices, and other parenting matters as a team, respecting each other's input.

Resolving Conflict with Love

Conflict is inevitable in any relationship. When disagreements arise, approach them with love, humility, and a commitment to finding solutions that benefit your family. When there are disagreements never involve your children in your disagreements.

INTIMACY AND ROMANCE

Maintain intimacy and romance in your marriage. Physical and emotional connection is vital to sustaining a healthy relationship.

Support Systems

Lean on your support systems, such as family, friends, or your church community, when needed. Don't hesitate to ask for help, allowing you both to have moments of rest and rejuvenation.

Balancing Roles

Balance your roles as parents and spouses. Remember that you were a couple before becoming parents, and nurturing your marriage remains a lifelong journey.

Seeking Professional Help

If you encounter significant challenges in your marriage, seek professional help. Pastors, counselors, or therapists can provide guidance and support during difficult times.

Renewing Your Commitment

Periodically renew your commitment to each other through renewal vows, anniversary celebrations, or other meaningful rituals. Reflect on your journey together and recommit to your marriage.

<u>In Summary</u>

- Strengthening marital bonds in Christian parenting is a vital aspect of nurturing a thriving family.
- Maintaining a marriage that provides love, security, and support throughout your child-rearing years can be achieved by working as a team.
- As your journey in Christian parenting continues, may your marriage serve as a beacon of God's love and grace, guiding your family through every season of life.

CHAPTER 19: THE LEGACY OF FAITHFUL PARENTING

Leaving a lasting impact on generations to come

As you near the conclusion of your journey in Christian parenting, it's essential to reflect on the legacy you are leaving for your children and future generations. This chapter explores the significance of the legacy of faithful parenting.

Understanding Legacy

Legacy is more than material wealth; it encompasses the values, beliefs, and principles you pass down to your children. Your legacy is a reflection of your faith, character, and the impact you make on those you influence.

Spiritual Inheritance

Your most significant legacy is the spiritual inheritance you leave for your children. It includes their faith in God, their understanding of Christian values, and their commitment to living out those values.

Intergenerational Blessings

A faithful parenting legacy extends beyond your immediate family. It can shape the lives of your grandchildren, great-grandchildren, and future generations, influencing them to walk in the path of faith.

Teaching by Example

The most powerful way to impart a legacy of faith is by living it out. Your children learn from your example, so model the values and principles you want them to embrace.

Family Traditions

Establish family traditions that reinforce your Christian values. These traditions create lasting memories and help instill a sense of identity rooted in faith.

Storytelling and Anecdotes

Share personal tales and stories that demonstrate the value of faith and the lessons you've learnt. These personal narratives can be powerful tools for teaching.

Creating a Family Mission Statement

Consider crafting a family mission statement that encapsulates your values, goals, and beliefs. Display it prominently in your home as a constant reminder.

Encouraging Service and Giving

Promote a legacy of service and giving by involving your family in charitable activities and missions work. Teach them the joy of helping others in the name of Christ.

Documenting Your Journey

Consider documenting your parenting journey through journals, videos, or letters to your children. These records can serve as a tangible reminder of your faith and love.

Continual Prayer

Pray for your children and their future regularly. Commit their lives and endeavors to God's care and guidance.

Passing Down Antique

Consider passing down meaningful antique, such as Bibles, crosses, or prayer journals, as tangible symbols of your faith legacy.

Embracing Grace

Acknowledge that no parent is perfect. Embrace God's grace for your own shortcomings and trust that His grace will continue to work in your children's lives.

<u>In Summary</u>

- The legacy of faithful parenting is a gift that keeps on giving. By understanding the importance of legacy as a parent you endeavor to leave a legacy of faith that will influence your family and generations to come.
- As you conclude this journey, may you find solace and joy in the knowledge that your faithful parenting has left an indelible mark on your family and the world.
- Your legacy is a testament to God's grace and love, and it will continue to shine brightly in the hearts of those you have nurtured.

CONCLUSION: EMPOWERING FAMILIES WITH FAITH

Guiding families toward a future rooted in Christian values

As we draw this journey of Christian parenting to a close, it's evident that faith plays a central role in shaping our families and the generations to come. We've explored the principles and practices that empower families with faith and the significance of these lessons cannot be overstated.

A Journey of Faith

Christian parenting is, at its core, a journey of faith. It's about trusting God to guide us as we nurture and raise our children. Through every season of life, from the joys of birth to the challenges of adolescence, our faith has been our anchor.

The Power of Prayer

Prayer is a powerful tool that empowers families. It connects us with God's wisdom and grace, providing strength and guidance in times of uncertainty. As parents, our prayers shape our children's lives, covering them with God's love and protection.

Building Strong Foundations

We've learned the importance of building strong foundations in our families. These foundations are rooted in love, communication, respect, and faith. They provide stability and security for our children as they navigate the complexities of the world.

The Role of Christian Values

Christian values are the bedrock of our parenting journey. They serve as our compass, guiding us as we teach our children about love, kindness, forgiveness, and compassion. These values shape our children's character and prepare them to be responsible, ethical, and loving individuals.

Fostering Inclusivity

Inclusivity has been a recurring theme in our discussions. We've explored how to create environments where every family member, regardless of age or ability, feels valued and included. Our faith calls us to embrace diversity and celebrate the unique gifts each family member brings.

Nurturing Spiritual Growth

We've seen that nurturing spiritual growth is not only about attending church but about living out our faith in our daily lives. Our families are places where faith is cultivated through prayer, Scripture, worship, and service.

STRENGTHENING MARITAL Bonds

Marriage is the foundation of our families. Strengthening our marital bonds is essential for providing a secure and loving environment for our kids. As we prioritize our marriages, we model healthy relationships and demonstrate the importance of commitment and love.

Leaving a Legacy

Finally, we've explored the idea of leaving a legacy of faith. Our parenting journey is not just about the here and now; it's about the impact we make on future generations. We've considered how our values, stories, and spiritual inheritance shape the legacy we leave behind.

A Future Rooted in Faith

Let us remember that our role as Christian parents extends beyond the boundaries of our homes. We are shaping the future, one child at a time, and empowering families with faith is our mission. Our families are beacons of God's love and grace, and they have the potential to impact the world with the transformative power of faith.

May your family continue to be a source of love, light, and inspiration to others. As you empower your family with faith, may you find strength, joy, and fulfillment in the knowledge that you are contributing to a future rooted in Christian values.

THIS WRAPS UP THE JOURNEY of Christian parenting by emphasizing the role of faith, the power of prayer, building strong foundations, the importance of Christian values, inclusivity, nurturing spiritual growth, strengthening marital bonds, and leaving a legacy. It encourages families to be beacons of God's love and grace and empowers them to impact the world with faith and Christian values.

Don't miss out!

Visit the website below and you can sign up to receive emails whenever patrick maina publishes a new book. There's no charge and no obligation.

https://books2read.com/r/B-A-TVPQ-ARUWD

BOOKS 2 READ

Connecting independent readers to independent writers.